# English 343: American Literature Since 1945

## Dr. Christina Bieber Lake

### Supplementary Course and Lecture Materials
### 1st edition

**Please bring this booklet to class everyday**
**2014: Caritas press**
**Copyright: Christina Bieber Lake**

## Why a college literature class? Why discussions in the classroom? Why not just read books on our own?

The assumptions that most students make about how we learn are, not surprisingly, the result of years of formal schooling. Because we have all been subjected to written examinations that require us to demonstrate what we have learned, we assume that the student who learns is rather like an empty cup that the teacher "pours" knowledge into. We tend to think of our education as the solitary gaining of facts or data, or as an understanding that comes, mysteriously, as the result of our remembering those facts or data for an exam.

But recent pedagogical research has illustrated that the assumption that knowledge is gained this way is erroneous. The research instead shows that the more active a student is in her education, the more she will learn. In other words, education is more about acquiring analytical skills and learning how to evaluate and handle ideas than it is about memorizing facts. The "cup" metaphor for the student implies that a student is passive and empty, and that the instructor will be the one to actively pour information into him. But teachers who teach by this model are in fact the *least* effective teachers, though they may (or may not) *know* the most. The main reason for this is that in this model, it is the teachers who are doing all the work. The result is ironic: the teacher *doubly* learns the material, but the student only gets a glimpse of what she sees, and then usually forgets it after a semester (or an hour!).

The better way to teach is for the instructor to facilitate a learning environment. That means that my responsibility as your teacher is to provide guidance, leadership, materials, and inspiration where and when I can. But the learning is up to you—and *must* be. Think about it this way: if the "cup" model were the best way to get an education, you would be wasting your time and your (and your parents') money in college. You could simply learn American literature by reading the novels and then reading one or two good critical works in the library. So what exactly do we gain by being in the classroom together? Let me suggest a few ideas.

1. Accountability. We know that we all tend to be lazy, even when it comes to our own education. So part of why you are here is the accountability of my assignments. But it is important that these assignments not be busy work. All of the assignments that I generate have been designed specifically to increase your involvement with the material we are reading together. Every time you are forced to focus and clarify your interpretive ideas in writing, such as in a BIR or a research essay, you actively learn. Every time you challenge yourself to engage in a conversation over someone else's BIR, you actively learn. Every time you read an outside critic's ideas and are forced to write a pithy summary, you actively learn. Every time you come to class ready to discuss a text and not just to hear about it, you actively learn. And most of all, when you have to get up in front of the class and lead other students into seeing what you have seen, you actively learn.

2. Other students. You will never fully recognize the value of having other intelligent students around you, reading, discussing, and writing about these same materials. It can be wonderfully motivating if you stop and think about this privilege. This is one of those things that makes the college experience irreplaceable.

3. My active feedback. There is one main difference between our discussion as a class and student bull sessions in the dorm: me! I **do** have ideas about the literature that have been forged from years of careful reading and study, and you will hear them. Do not think that because I lead by discussion that you will not hear what I think! I cannot help but respond to students' ideas—both in class, and in response to written work. I am also available during office hours or for lunch if you want to exchange ideas further.

I think it is time to think of a new way to think about our class time and the time you spend outside of class preparing for it. Don't forget that as a general guideline, you should be devoting **at least three hours outside this class to every hour spent in it**. Some weeks it will be more than that, some, less. What you get out of the class is directly related to what you put into it, which is one of the many reasons why it is important to not take too many credit hours per semester. If you find yourself overloaded this semester, do not be afraid to drop this class and take it again later.

But more important, I would like to encourage you to pray about trying to get your motivation from learning, not from grades. Literature teaches us a number of intangible things; it would be a real shame to let those things pass you by while you are worrying about how to keep up your GPA. Please do not think that I am trying to send you a double message. The college requires me to give grades, and I try to give them responsibly, by *gradating* between students as fairly as possible. But it is up to you to keep grades in perspective within your spiritual life—a big task. If you need further incentive to get away from the meaningless grade grind, consider this: career services recently reported that employers ranked the potential employee's GPA at number 13 in a list of what they were looking for in the people they hired. What ranked in the top three? First was communication skills, both oral and written. Second was the ability to work on team. Third was honesty and reliability. I encourage you to pray and ask God which of these three areas you should strive to grow in, because this class will give you an opportunity to exercise all of them as we explore contemporary American literature together. Chances are very good that you won't really care what your grade was in this class ten years from now, but if you are open to it, you might learn a skill or encounter an idea that will change your life. So please: trust God for your future, and let's try to move beyond grades and learn something truly significant!

Class *lectio divina*

Dr. Christina Bieber Lake

Ideas and quotations from *Lectio Divina: Renewing the Ancient Practice of Praying the Scriptures*, by M. Basil Pennington. Crossroad, 1998.

*Lectio* means reading, and so *lectio divina* simply means a kind of reading of God. In the early church it was associated with hearing the word of God spoken aloud. It is a practice of slowing down over the scripture, repeating the words, so that the words enmesh with our souls in a way that is deeper than a merely intellectual understanding.

Pennington writes that there are 4 major parts, each of which can be compared to aspects of an intimate personal relationship with God. The point of this comparison is to remind us that these words are spoken by God to us *in relationship with us*. This fact is surprisingly easy to forget as we study scripture.

1. *Lectio* (reading). Acquaintanceship. Suggests position of being open to transformation by someone and something new.

2. *Meditatio* (meditation). Friendly companionship. Usually this involves a simple repeating of the words that capture your attention. This is not meant to be primarily an intellectual exercise, but a surrendering to the text, a being-with the text.

3. *Oratio* (speaking response, dialogue). Friendship. A prayerful response by us; we talk to God in a more give-and-take way.

4. *Contemplatio* (settling in with the truth, contemplation). Union. We become fully present to the One who is eternally present to us.

Why is this exercise so important? Consider the following:

*The speed of our information age, and how it mitigates against this kind of hearing.

*The insidious temptation to think that *more* is *better*.

*How easy it is for one's intellect to become a barrier to this kind of transformation.


Pennington:

"One of the things that can most undermine our actual practice of *lectio* is a subtle or not-so-subtle boredom that seems to say 'I've heard all this before.'" (7)


"The most basic foolishness we can be dominated by is the foolishness of self-satisfaction. All of life is a coming out of ignorance into the light of fuller understanding." (15)


So I recommend that, as a class, we let the words of the scripture sink in to our souls as they are repeated week after week. Do not think you need to fully understand the meaning, and do not close your mind off to a potentially new understanding because you think "I've heard this before."

## Assignment specifics and student models

The following pages contain my specific instructions regarding the class assignments as well as actual papers that I have collected from previous students in my classes. I am providing these models to you not because they are perfect (they are not), but because they are examples of the kind of work that I view as **extraordinary** or **outstanding**. The grade of "A" is supposed to be reserved for this kind of product. I would remind you again that how hard a student works does not necessarily indicate what kind of grade that student will receive. These students were rewarded both for having original insights *and* for writing clearly and effectively.

As you read them, please pay attention to the following skills that I have a tendency to weigh most heavily:

1. **The central insight as translated into a thesis**. How does the student make an argument, rather than just an observation? How is it focused on a narrow enough idea? What makes it compel you to keep reading?

2. **Close reading of the text**. It is care with the text that separates the discipline of English from other disciplines. The text should be viewed as the central aspect of analysis, not a springboard into some other analysis or as simple support for ideas. How does the student quote and analyze the text with care instead of "prooftexting"?

3. **Writing style**. How is the paper organized so as to move logically from one point to the next? How does the student show dexterity with language?

4. **Mechanics**. How does the paper adhere to standard grammar as well as to MLA style conventions? (Please be advised that the format has been changed to fit this book. Your work must follow the format I outline. Student papers should always be left margin justified, for example, and are to be double-spaced unless otherwise instructed).

## Guidelines: Brief Interpretive Response (BIR)

1. The purpose of the brief interpretive response is to demonstrate your ability to perform an **insightful, close, analytical, and interpretive reading** of a text that is interesting and provokes class discussion. The response should begin straight away with the assertion that you want to make. **Your paper should not exceed 650 words.** You should be wary of trying to do too much—narrow and deep is best here. Always quote from the text and analyze what you quote. Please see the student models available in this booklet.

2. Bring 10 copies of your BIR (formatted to fit one page only please!) to class on the day to which you are assigned.

3. Your final copy of the BIR is due exactly one week after your in-class presentation date **at the start of class. This should be a double-spaced copy (headed by your name, Eng 343, date, word count) for me to evaluate.**

3. **One visit to the writing center is required for either the BIR OR the summary of critical work (you may, of course, go for both).** This requires advanced planning. As always, I encourage you to start early and give your writing a cooling off period. **Do not be misled: short papers are very difficult to write.** Leave yourself time to revise. You are always welcome to bring a draft into an appointment with me.

4. When you read your paper to your group, read slowly and clearly. Have a question or two ready to begin discussion.

5. Listeners: mark errors in the text, and underline what you want to ask about or discuss as a class. It is your responsibility to help continue the discussion. At the end of the time, assign a number to each of the four criteria and write one sentence of explanation. Your evaluation will be kept anonymous.

# BIR: Criteria for Evaluation

1. **Depth and accuracy of interpretation and analysis:**

    *Powerful, original, and well-supported = 7

    *Believable and well-supported = 6

    * Average (ho-hum) and fairly well-supported = 5

    *Not well-supported and/or irresponsible = 3/4

2. **Ability of interpretation to provoke discussion:**

    *We couldn't wait to talk about it = 7

    *Interested us strongly = 6

    *We already thought about these ideas / not much help = 5

    *Boring/irrelevant to key issues = 3/4

3. **Quality of writing:**

    *Compelling, well-organized, and error-free = 7

    *Clear, reasonably organized, and error-free = 6

    *Minor errors and/or somewhat unclear = 5

    *Major errors and/or unclear or disorganized = 3/4

4. **Oral presentation of ideas:**

    *Read clearly, excellent follow-up = 7

    *Read clearly, adequate follow-up = 6

    *Read reasonably well, average follow up = 5

    *Read poorly and/or did not follow up = 3/4

Remember that the grade of 7 should be given only to **exceptional work.** Although I am the final arbiter of grades, I do consult peer assessments of your work. Usually there is substantial agreement between my assessment and peer assessment.

Josephine Model Student

English 343

Sept 24, 1914

Word count: 545


By alluding to the Biblical account of Jacob's struggle with an angel of the Lord (Genesis 32:22-32), Denise Levertov, in her poem "Where is the Angel?," shows the speaker's longing to shatter the glass and sunder the iron that surrounds and protects her from the "outside, [where] the stark shadows menace" (ll. 4-5) in exchange for a greater, more tangible experience with God, and a world that is no longer soundless.

In "Where is the Angel?," the speaker's feeling of confinement in a lukewarm world is evident as a result of Levertov's use of phrases which imply a lack of extremes. Trapped inside the "glass bubble" (l. 2), the speaker breathes the "tepid aid" (l. 7) of a "mild September" (l. 3), sees only the "blur of asters" (ll. 7-8) through a "gentle haze" (l. 14), and hears only the gold-dust's "murmur" (l. 9), rather than a shout or a whisper. The speaker does not deny that this world is pleasant, but is still not satisfied with such an even-keel pleasantness and therefore expresses a yearning for an angel with whom to wrestle. In light of Jacob's wrestling match with the Lord – an experience during which Jacob sees God face to face – the request for an angel to wrestle is, in essence, a request for a deeply intense experience with the Lord. This experience is so important to the speaker that even safety and comfort can be discarded. If the glass shatters, it will no longer keep the world out, and if the iron sunders, the heart may be more vulnerable, but the speaker sees these "protective devices" as only a hindrance in his or her quest for God.

Not only does the speaker in Levertov's poem want to have an experience like Jacob's; the speaker also desires to carry the mark of such a passion-filled struggle. During Jacob's fight, the angel of the Lord "touched the socket of

Jacob's hip on the sinew of the thigh," and as a result, all could see Jacob's limp when the sun rose the next day. For the speaker in "Where is the Angel?," the renewed presence of sound in a world which has had the "volume turned off" (l. 16) would be indicative of one's struggle with an angel, or a struggle with similar magnitude. In her poem, Levertov renders the speaker soundless and mutes the world, reducing all noise to a murmur and quieting stark shadows so that they are unheard. As a result, the speaker cries out, "Where is the angel to wrestle with me and wound not my thigh but my throat, so curses and blessings flow storming out…?" (ll. 21-24).

The speaker desires for his or her reclaimed voice to be the equivalent of Jacob's limp – physical evidence of an experience with God. However, this leaves the reader to question, what is the purpose of this reclaimed voice? Does the speaker intend to use this new-found voice to share truth with the world outside the glass bubble - truth which had been previously trapped *inside* the glass bubble with the speaker? Or is the demand for an angel with whom to wrestle only an effort to live life on the edge and perhaps earn a few impressive battle scars?

Angela McClain

English 343

September 24, 2050

Word Count: 600

Eat More ~~Chikin~~ ChickieNobs

In *Oryx and Crake*, seemingly cute brand names exemplify and further cultural desensitization by substituting simulacra for reality. Even an apparently innocent moniker like "ChickieNobs Gourmet Dinners" represents something synthetic which has essentially replaced reality. Jimmy /Snowman and others may long for actual chicken, but the culture as a whole celebrates the march of progress which has left (relatively) organic animal products behind. Similarly, although BlyssPluss—which serves as a sexual aid, prophylactic, and elixir of youth—produces horrific side effects in clinical trials (295), the initially skeptical Jimmy becomes enthusiastic when he realizes its marketing potential. He does ask, as a matter of curiosity, where Crake procures the subjects for his trials. When Crake replies that his subjects come from "the poorer countries" and "the ranks of the desperate, as usual," Jimmy shows no shock or indignation but instead asks, "Where do I fit in?" (296). One might speculate that Snowman, recalling this scene later, feels appalled or at least regretful, but Atwood does not explicitly offer his reaction. Rather, she artfully places upon the reader the onus of responding with horror or indifference. The reader may either recoil appropriately or fantasize about the product's promises of augmented bliss.

Atwood's cultural portrait becomes even more dismally familiar when she uses brand names to show her characters' desensitization to matters concerning the beginning and end of life. Ramona, Jimmy's stepmother, shows no particular concern about her failed attempts to conceive since "If nothing 'natural' happened soon, she said, they'd try 'something else' from one of the agencies— Infantade, Foetility, Perfectababe, one of those" (250). Her apparent confidence demonstrates her cultural heedlessness about the origins of life.* She seems to possess in small measure the utter disregard Jimmy's father has for the physical character of humanity: in a fight with his first wife, he asserts, "It's just proteins, you know that! There's nothing sacred about cells and tissue" (57). Brand names, which permeate his world, eventually lead to Jimmy's similar desensitization to human life. Jimmy spends his adolescence playing such flippantly brutal computer games as Kwiktime Osama and Blood and Roses, in which players trade historical atrocities and works of art according to terrifyingly precise exchange rates (77-79). These brand-name games' triviality soon deadens Jimmy to the extent that he seeks out hedsoff.com, a site showing actual, live executions. These executions take place in Asia, of course, because the brand names' desensitizing effect relies on a distancing of subject from object: "I-thou" must become "I-it." The distancing may be figurative—as when great globular organs replace breathing, squawking chickens—or literal, as when Jimmy begins frequenting hedsoff.com and HottTotts. Jimmy gives no thought to the harm he may be inflicting on others by visiting a cutely named site like HottTotts. He bears no ill will toward its far-away victims: "He'd meant well, or at least he hadn't meant ill. He'd never wanted to hurt anyone, not seriously, not in real space-time. Fantasies didn't count" (284). Yet fantasies do count, as he finds when he comes to love the victimized Oryx too late to save her from violent death. They have real effects even when they are cleverly packaged as innocent simulacra.

Ultimately, this debasement by brand name brings about the destruction of Jimmy's entire world, which finds the brand-name allurement so seductive that its deadliness goes unnoticed. The brand-name products promise meat without chickens, babies without biology, violence without blood, and brutal sex without violation. This kind of world—where marketed fantasies profane reality by objectifying and trivializing it—necessarily ends in an all-too-real violence, strewn with the bodies its culture debased.

\* Clarification: As one whose appearance on the world stage was by no means a surprise, this author does not wish to criticize fertility aids as such. Without them, the universe would be bereft of at least one brilliant, yet humble mind.

John Nathanael Coffman

English 343

September 24, 2070

Word count: 647

 

The ending of "Parker's Back" comes as a shock: in an attempt to please his religiously fanatic wife, Sarah Ruth, O.E. Parker applies a tattoo of Christ to his back. However, instead of this pleasing her as the reader expects he is beaten by her for his efforts. His wife's rejection would appear to be O'Connor repudiation of Parker's burgeoning sense of the divine in favor of Sarah Ruth's spirit based theology, but what O'Connor is actually rejecting in her ending is Sarah Ruth's theological vision of an inhuman Christ. The act of violence meted out to Parker is not meant by O'Connor to shown an error; it is rather the last step that brings his character to what O'Connor believes to be the true Christian experience: metaphysical guidance (Parker's "instinct") and shared suffering with Christ.

Despite being described as a "hawk-eyed angel" (426) and constantly being attributed "religious" scruples, Sarah Ruth is not the religious paragon she would appear to be. Her absent father is symbolic for her absent sense of her heavenly father: she defines Christ as a purely spiritual being. It is she, not Parker, who is spiritually blind. Her blindness subtly manifests itself in her inability to recognize images: she mistakes a chicken for an "eagle" (429) and most tellingly when faced with Parker's Christ tattoo she states that "'It ain't anybody I know" (442). This characterization is not nearly as prominent as her observations on how Parker seems to be wasting his life getting one tattoo after another. Her religious flaws are subsumed by her husband's tattoo related foibles which distract the reader from her flaws. His tattoo addiction, however, is the force that is drawing Parker closer to the divine than Sarah Ruth.

Parker is the sort of man who obeys his "instincts;" they prompt his tattoo habit, his joining the navy, and marriage. This "instinct" is O'Connor's insinuation of divine guidance which has led Parker through all the stages of his life and stands contrary to Sarah Ruth's sense of the divine, which is rootless. His "instinct" is what attracted him to tattoos. O'Connor uses the religiously charged language of "blindness" and "direction" when she describes how tattoos turned him, a "blind boy… [in] so gently in a different direction that he did not know his destination had been changed" (427). This direction culminates in the application of the tattoo of Christ which seems to be a misguided gesture in a life apparently misspent. However, the "instinct" which has guided him has not failed him. By binding Christ to his flesh he begins to share in Christ's suffering; his "instinct," is revealed to have been divine guidance. Crawling home to his wife, Parker breaks down and whispers his name, Obadiah Elihue, in order to be let in and "all at once he felt the light pouring through him, turning his spider web soul into a perfect arabesque of colors, a garden of trees and birds and beasts" (441). O'Connor's imagery here shows that by accepting his biblically rich name, Obadiah Elihue, he is coming closer to a religious breakthrough.

The viciousness of the beating Parker receives from his wife when she rejects his tattoo knocks him "senseless and [raises] large welts on the face of the tattooed Christ" (442). Sarah Ruth's act of violence serves as the final step in which Parker comes to share directly in Christ's suffering with his body receiving blows that echo Christ's Passion. This action validates his "instincts" as being divine in nature contrary to his wife's Gnostic beliefs. Parker's religious journey is rooted in a Catholic understanding of the role of physical pain, metaphysical "instinct," and shared suffering. In the end, clutching the pecan tree as if it were the cross, he is vindicated; Sarah Ruth is not because in her Gnostic viciousness she does not mete out righteous indignation but rather cruel unbelief.

# Guidelines: Summary of Critical Work

1. The purpose of this assignment is to test your ability to read, understand, and summarize a secondary critical source.

2. Your task will be to select one book length critical study **OR** two related journal articles that you will read carefully and summarize in four or five pages (900-1300 words, double spaced). **Do not exceed the word count limit.** Use the **MLA bibliography research database (available on-line through the library's web page)** to locate your choices, and start early as our library's collection is limited and will not yield the best sources. **You must clear your secondary source/s with me two weeks before your presentation. You may do this by e-mail, but you MUST bring in at least three possible titles for secondary sources and include author, publisher and published date for each. If you are trying to do related articles, you will need at least six choices (three possible pairings).** The reason for this is to help me to determine whether that source is worth reading and summarizing.

3. Your summary must include your best guess as to the theoretical approach the critic/s have taken. To learn about basic theoretical approaches to the study of literature, you will need to read either Culler, *Literary Theory, a Very Short Introduction* (Oxford) (see especially the appendix), or for more detail: *A Handbook of Critical Approaches to Literature.* (Oxford). These books are available in the bookstore. I suggest you begin to read now. Also note: the more diverse sources your group chooses among yourselves, the better.

3. Brief summaries are very difficult to write. Note well: I am not asking for an *evaluation* of the argument—you are not really qualified yet to do that. You should not waste space with a snazzy introduction, but instead begin with a thesis that best characterizes the heart of the argument. You should then move to a structure that enables you to illustrate the main areas of argument and to give a short quotation or two that can serve as a pithy example of the critic's argumentation.

5. **This critical summary will be due on the day of your presentation. If you are not on time to class, the paper is late.** I expect to grant no extensions. (Though this deadline might be difficult, please understand that this work is supposed to help you with your presentation, so it is less helpful to turn it in later. I recommend, as always, starting much earlier).

6. As there is very little formal writing required, I expect grammatical perfection and will grade these as closely as any other writing assignment (NB: I'm relentless…). As always, MLA format is expected. Double space your work. Consult the student models for examples.

7. **One visit to the writing center is required for either this assignment OR the BIR (or both).** If you do not visit the writing center (they send me notification), your grade will be lowered.

# Guidelines: Group Presentation

1. Your research in preparing for this presentation should involve no fewer than **five outside, refereed sources** (i.e., no web sites except for general info which you should check against refereed sources). This should be easy if you each choose different sources for your summaries.

2. Your group will be entirely responsible for the **first 40 minutes** of class time. Please begin with the class *lectio divina* (your time begins after the reading ends). How you use the time is up to you, keeping in mind that your presentation should 1) contribute to our understanding of the text, author and period; 2) reflect what you learned in your research; 3) engage the interest of the class; 4) include a compelling handout (one page only) that you photocopy for each class member. The handout should evince signs of outside research and textual sensitivity.

3. Groups may decide how to break up the time. Some groups may want to have each person present his or her research and then lead a discussion, others may want to work together as a group to develop other visual aids, use drama, set up a debate, etc. Be creative and resist a lazy solution; for example, while you may employ video resources, it would not be the best use of time to simply show a movie. It is not necessarily a bad idea to follow other groups' ideas, but do not just default to what has gone on before! DO NOT EXCEED 40 MINUTES. IT IS YOUR RESPONSIBILITY TO STOP ON TIME OR YOUR GROUP'S GRADE WILL BE AFFECTED. The time usually goes by faster than you think that it will.

4. The presentation will be evaluated (by me, with input from the class) according to the quality of its content, the use of strategies that actively engage the learners, the effectiveness of its presentation style, your cohesiveness as a group, the quality of the handout, and so on. I am available to advise groups about research and teaching plans provided that you make arrangements well in advance of the presentation.

5. An outline of your presentation and a works consulted list is due (at the latest) the *class period before* your presentation day. This may be submitted to me via e-mail. The primary reason for this deadline is to help me to plan the remaining class time on your text.

6. **Do not use materials in this book!** You usually get to go first on any given text we study so that I will not steal your thunder. Don't steal mine!

# Model summary of a critical work:  book

Kristin Niehof

English 343

September 24, 1930

Word count: 943


Cavell, Stanley. *The Senses of Walden.* New York: The Viking
Press, 1972.  Print.


      The reader of *Walden* has a tough job.  He must
decide how to integrate nature passages with philosophical
discourses, social commentaries with animal observations.
Cavell, taking a formalistic approach, opens with the
hypothesis that the book is complete in itself; interpretation
should stay within the bounds of the text.  The "senses" are
the multiple levels of meaning that the reader must realize.
Cavell posits that *Walden* is Thoreau's attempt to, through
these senses, redeem both language and human life.

      Cavell builds the first chapter around this thesis:
*Walden* is a new scripture for the new America, and as such it
requires the rebirth of the reader.  Cavell takes Thoreau's
reference to the "father tongue" in which he composed the
book as an indication of the conditions for reading it. This
religious language indicates that the reader must be born anew
in order to fully understand the text, just as a believer must
undergo baptism before he can comprehend the Bible.
Thoreau's (and the reader's) baptism is "immersion not in the
water but in the book of Walden" (17). A second
manifestation of the book's "father tongue" is its prophetic
nature.  As prophecy is the language of God the Father, so is
*Walden*.  The writer's role is to awaken people, as the prophet
does, to the consequences of their wrong actions. (The
symbol of the cock-crow strengthens this analogy.) Once the

reader is baptized, awakened, and able to wholly dedicate himself to the full senses of words, he will redeem language.

In addition to the language of the prophets, *Walden* also borrows the scriptural language of parables. The strongest and most complex parable of the book is the chapter about the bean field. In one level of this parable Thoreau equates his hoeing with the actions of Achilles before Troy: "filling up the trenches with weedy dead." Cavell writes that this is a parody of parable-making: "What the writer is mocking in the obviousness of this parable is parable-making itself, those moralizings over nature that had become during the past century a literary pastime, and with which his writing would be confused" (21). The highest sense of the bean field parable is that hoeing is a trope for writing. The farmer tries to make the soil express itself in bean plants just as the writer tries to make words express themselves in truths. Thoreau shows his dedication to all senses of language (both the lower, literal "mother tongue" and the exalted "father tongue") in that he takes the literal role of the farmer as well as the role of the writer. The parable extends even beyond this to become part of a theory of language. By the simple but significant act of relating writing to farming, Thoreau argues that books are part of nature, and nature expresses itself in them. This relationship with nature heightens the value of words.

In the second chapter Cavell contends that Thoreau uses questions as a beginning point in his quest to redeem human life. He writes that "his problem . . . is to get us to ask the questions, and then to show us that we do not know what we are asking, and then to show us that we have the answer" (46). These questions grow out of loss, a major theme in the book. Thoreau keeps our choices in front of us, reminding us at every step what we have chosen and what we have lost. This causes us to ask questions and realize that we "have lost the world, i.e. are lost to it" (51).

The theme of loss modulates in the third chapter into the idea of outsideness, which is central to Thoreau's philosophy. Cavell argues that when Thoreau sees a double shadow of himself on the ice, he is experiencing "the absolute awareness of self without embarrassment—consciousness of self, and of the self's standing, beyond self-consciousness" (101). Cavell holds this up as the doctrine that this scripture puts forth. A man must get outside of society and beyond even himself before he can evaluate and then redeem his life. Thoreau lives this out literally by moving to the woods, and he lives it on many other levels by watching himself and observing his own actions as closely as he does the animals'. The philosophy of determinism comes in here; Thoreau sees that men believe that they determine themselves and have no choices left. The image he uses for this determinism is the train, which is fated to run the same track every day. The way to get beyond this degraded rut of life is to become watchmen or guardians of ourselves. We must change and be open to spring and to awakening; only then can we redeem our lives.

Cavell meets the challenge of integrating the sections of *Walden* by treating them all as having multiple senses. The words must be true literally (the mother tongue—Thoreau really did go to the woods) and figuratively (the father tongue—Thoreau lived outside of society and himself). By forcing the reader to ask questions, Thoreau makes him realize that he is determining himself and doesn't have to do so. The reader recognizes that he has the answers to the questions he has just asked. When the reader takes words (and their meanings) seriously and fully dedicates himself to the implications of his beliefs, he will redeem both himself and language. This redemption is what Thoreau set out to achieve in his two years at Walden and in his literary account of them.

# Model summary of a critical work:  two articles

Elle Morgan

English 343

September 24, 1871

Word count: 1020

Powers, Peter Kerry.  "Scribbling for a Life: Masculinity, Doctrine, and Style in the Work of John Updike." *Christianity and Literature* 43.3-4 (1994): 329-346. Print.

Robinson, Sally.  "'Unyoung, Unpoor, Unblack': John Updike and the Construction of Middle American Masculinity." *Modern Fiction Studies* 44.2 (1998): 331-363. Print.

The Shifting Role of Masculinity in the World of John Updike

To an uninformed reader, the racism and sexism that pervades much of John Updike's writing might look like nothing more than the outraged cry of a white chauvinist. On the contrary, Peter Kerry Powers and Sally Robinson, offering criticism from the gender studies movement, argue that Updike's treatment of blacks and women is indicative of the shifting role of masculinity in the 1960s and 1970s.

In his essay, "Scribbling for a Life: Masculinity, Doctrine, and Style in the Work of John Updike," Powers defends the overt sexism in Updike's work as the "result of changing circumstances in the practice of writing and the shifting metaphors for gender difference in the twentieth century" (330). He begins his criticism by reviewing the Enlightenment view of the writer as an imitator of God; both create with unlimited creativity and authority over their realms and both are traditionally thought of as male.  The turn of the century heralded industrial capitalism, turning writing from an act of authoritative creation into a mechanized trade. For Updike, "writing is no longer the great self- and male-affirming activity that it at least once pretended to be" (333). The intricacies of dealing with this loss of meaning and manhood can be seen through two of his fictional characters, Henry Bech of *Bech: A Book* and Thomas Marshfield of *A Month of Sundays*.

Through Bech, Powers argues, Updike illustrates the demise of literary paternity. At one point in the story, Bech finds himself a part of a sorry collection of emasculated, decaying male writers dominated by one monumental, virile woman author. Rather than viewing this as a bitter attack on the cultural dominance of women, Powers see it as Updike's acknowledgement of his membership among the "de-masculinized," mechanized sphere of modern writing.

Thomas Marshfield also illustrates the demise of the independent masculine creator as he is "forced to write at the behest of a female overseer" (339). As a last effort to retain his masculinity, Marshfield turns to the strong prose of Karl Barth, hoping to find a God who "stands apart – wholly other, dependent upon no one, immune to claims by anyone" (340). Updike, like Marshfield, was a disciple of Barth. However, although Updike's writing might appear to be dominated by the "Barthian phallus," that vein of theology is often trumped in his writing by a love of nature and details, leading Powers to believe that Updike was searching for a more personal, loving God.

In conclusion, Powers maintains that Updike's apparent sexism is rooted in deep nostalgia for a time when the idea of masculinity dominated the world of literature and theology. Rather than dismissing Updike as an oppressive male author, it is valuable to read him as one of the early literary pioneers struggling to make sense of a new American definition of masculinity.

In her article, "'Unyoung, Unpoor, Unblack': John Updike and the Construction of Middle American Masculinity," Robinson dives more specifically into the particulars of the civil rights and sexual liberation movements as a means of explaining the sexism in Updike's writing. The sixties and seventies, she argues, were a time of revolutionary change in which the middle-class white American male shifted from being the norm to becoming the enemy of change and liberation.

In the first section of her essay, Robinson maps the discovery of the white male "Middle American" during the 1960s. "What defines Middle American white men in this period is a sense that they have lost what was rightfully theirs" (335). In this decade, race is the predominate issue. Class and gender differences faded, uniting the victimized white Middle Americans against the "young, poor, and black." Middle Americans struggled greatly with the tension between the traditional American values of individualism and autonomy and their identity as a group. Powers quotes George Lipsizt who says, "an ideology and a language of liberal individualism have secured white dominance while hiding the fact that white Americans benefit in untold ways from their membership in a group" (341). This tension, Powers argues, plays a central role in the crisis of white masculinity.

Updike sheds light on the shifting role of the white middle class American through his *Rabbit* novels. However, he adds complexity to an already difficult issue by imbuing Rabbit with both a desire to reassert his manhood and a desire to retain his disempowerment to aid in the development of a new white male identity. In *Rabbit Redux*, Updike creates a sense of the white body as bland, worn out by technology, and weak in comparison to the virile, natural bodies of black men. Rabbit's feminist wife, Janie, criticizes his declining body, linking white decline to the women's movement. Rabbit's emasculation is further emphasized by the fact that he didn't fight in Vietnam and can only feed off of other people's stories. These racial, gender, and political forces combine to drive Rabbit into an overwhelming emotional darkness from which Updike provides no sanctuary.

Robinson focuses the third part of her essay on Updike's *Rabbit is Rich*. In this novel, "Harry is freed of the necessity to assume, or own up to, the racial identity forced upon him in *Rabbit Redux*. This freedom is bought, quite literally, by Harry's new wealth" (351). The seventies, Robinson argues, offered money as a means of escape from the darkness that Updike had previously painted. Rather than pining after blackness, Rabbit can now satisfy his desire for it by buying South African gold coins or Caribbean vacations. Also emphasized in this novel is Rabbit's fascination with sexual penetration of the male body. Robinson argues that this "fearful fascination with violation of bodily boundaries" (353) is reflective of the state of affairs in American politics during the seventies, as Updike views America as a masculine construct. The novel portrays America's foreign policy, like its men, as impotent and penetrated.

Robinson concludes by observing, "Rabbit's envy of the racial and sexual others who have changed the shape of his world suggests that, for Updike, the invisibility of white masculinity is, at best, a mixed blessing" (359). For Rabbit and the other white American men of the sixties and seventies, their disempowerment due to political, gender, and racial shifts forced them to define a new identity for themselves.

Note to students: sometimes I require a research essay in my classes. The following model is included for that reason.

**Model Research Essay: Michelle Augustine**

Fade to Black and White: Color and Sexuality in Toni
Morrison's *The Bluest Eye*

When Toni Morrison first published *The Bluest Eye* in 1970, the novel addressed a contemporary problem strangling American society: the whitewashing and objectification of black culture by white social norms, especially standards of beauty. In a recent *Chicago Tribune* article entitled "Setting the Standards," journalist Tracy Mack investigates the residual effects of—and reactions against—this phenomenon. According to Mack, the research of DePaul's Midge Wilson indicates that middle- and upper-class black women living in largely white areas "are more likely to have a Eurocentric outlook about their self-image…while those who live in predominantly African-American or minority neighborhoods tend to subscribe to traditional Afrocentric ideals of beauty;" Wilson notes that "black women [of upper and middle classes] may be succumbing to messages of European cultures" (8.1). Mack and Wilson make it clear that black women's conception of their own beauty and "sexiness" has increased to exceed— by several times—white women's belief in *their* beauty, but the problems fleshed out in *The Bluest Eye* remain central and ominous in black circles. Morrison's Pauline, who falls easy prey to impossible white standards of attractiveness, fully denies her beauty and sexuality at the novel's close; she, in fact, rejects sex and physicality in favor of a dry, white notion of beauty. Morrison shifts from vibrantly colorful descriptions of Pauline's life and sexuality to grim, colorless images of the black Pauline's bootless interactions with white society. As Pauline moves from sexuality to asexuality, the wide color spectrum representing her life drains to a black-and-white dichotomy.

Morrison uses pre-Lorrain Pauline to investigate black female sexuality in a relatively 'untouched' state. While still insulated from white influence, Pauline remains categorically unlike Mr. Henry's ex-wife; armed with a singular and satisfied self-consciousness, Pauline *does* "smell like a woman" and is not "just too clean" (13). Even before describing the first encounter with Cholly, Morrison defines Pauline's life in sexual terms. Sex is Pauline's religion. Though her mental intentions lie in scripture and hymns, "her body tremble[s] for redemption" (113); a devout believer, she awaits the eschatological advent of some sexual "Presence," an "all-embracing tenderness...wordless knowing and ...soundless touching" (113). This "Presence"—the fulfillment of her sexual expectations—takes the form of Cholly. It is no coincidence that the sexualized Pauline best verbally asserts herself in her monologue describing the couple's conjugal relationship. Their sexual interaction is the most certain and recognizable locus of Pauline's personal presence: "I be strong, I be pretty, I be young" (130). Here, in her sexuality, she finds and rejoices in her personhood, as exhibited by the repetition of self reference in the monologue: "*Not until I feel him loving me. Just me. Sinking into me...That he would die rather than take his thing out of me. Of me. Not until he has let go of all he has, and give it to me. To me. To me*" (130). Pauline's confidence in her existence derives from confidence in her sexuality.

With Cholly's arrival, sex slides from the fuzzy arena of dream and aspiration into an extant world of vibrant color. Before her full initiation into sexuality, the young Pauline had been "enchanted by numbers and depressed by words;" she "missed—without knowing what she missed—paints and crayons" (111). Morrison—vis-à-vis Pauline—describes Cholly in "paints and crayons," employing myriad sensual "bits of color" in the rapturous portrayal of their first encounter (115). Pauline, bearing the "thwarted soul of an artist" (Pettis 29), creates a scintillating palette of hues from a life culminating in Cholly. She renders the promise of sexual interaction in the purple "deep inside [her]"—the purple that clings to her hips, her dress, her soul—the "cool and yellowish" hue of lemonade, and the "streak of green" of

summer june bugs. The artist represented herself in color—
and in the hope for sex: *So when Cholly come up and tickled my
foot, it was like them berries, that lemonade, them streaks of green the
june bugs made, all come together.* (115) Potential becomes
actuality in Pauline and Cholly's sexual relationship. Pauline's
artist soul inevitably reaches for color as a metaphor for sex
and describes it in pulsating technicolor: *"I begin to feel those
little bits of color floating up into me—deep in me. That streak of green
from the june-bug light, the purple from the berries trickling along my
thighs, Mama's lemonade yellow runs sweet in me. Then I feel like I'm
laughing between my legs, and the laughing gets all mixed up with the
colors…"* (131). Significantly, the description remains devoid
of the two hues—black and white—that dominate the novel.
Against a black southern backdrop, sex is "rainbow all inside"
(131), a spectrum, a palette; and Pauline equates her sexuality
with a vibrant, colorful presence of self.

In a quintessential migration northward, Pauline
begins to replace the lushly colorful sensuality of the South
with the dry, absolutist gnosticism of small-town mid-
America. Lorrain, ironically the "melting pot on the lip of
America" (117), forces interaction with a dominant culture she
can neither understand nor join. She "[isn't] much used to so
much white folks…they [are] everywhere—next door,
downstairs, all over the streets" (117), and their metaphysical
influence is as ubiquitous as their physical presence. Lorrain's
black women have adopted white standards of appearance and
condescend to ridicule Pauline's countrification. When her
attempts at acceptable beauty fail, desperate self-
dissatisfaction edges out proactive self-appreciation, and she
"merely want[s] other women to cast favorable glances her
way" (118). The white-controlled social climate demands full
acquiescence of body, mind, and soul, and Pauline cannot
withstand its requirements. She successfully rejects her first
white employer's insistence that she abandon Cholly, but the
encounter remains one in a series that erodes the fabric of
her—especially physical—self-satisfaction. Morrison
sexualizes the showdown— *"When I got outside, I felt pains in my
crotch, I had held my legs together so tight trying to make that woman
understand"* [121]). The event and events surrounding it

irreversibly construct a race-defined wall between Pauline and her own physical comfort.

Caucasian culture and social climate do not merely blanch individuals' notion of beauty and, as Anne Spencer writes, "[turn] the blood in a ruby rose/To a poor white poppy flower" ("White Things"); they effectively dichotomize lovely white from its inevitable polar opposite. Instead of the diversity of colors she so prizes (Spencer's "golden stars with lances fine...hills all red and darkened pine"), Pauline's "education in the movies" offers blotches of black and white (122). In a black room, assaulted by enormous black and white images prescribing a rubric for beauty (a beauty, incidentally, totally unconnected with any concept of black sexuality), Pauline is helpless; her vibrancy, her "rainbow," inevitably dissolves into self-critical absolutism. The ideals of physical beauty and romantic love, once fluid with a vibrant hope for the "Presence," now rupture and shrivel into "the most destructive ideas in the history of human thought" (122). The effect is sexual as well as cognitive; Morrison, writes Jane Kuenz, describes "the effect of [media's images of "femininity"] on women themselves *on the level of the body* and in terms of how they understand and experience their own sexuality" (426). The physical results of Pauline's interaction with movies characterize her cathexion of the black-white dichotomy. "On the level of the body," she recognizes her blackness and the "otherness" of screen actresses.

Until her addiction to the silver screen, Pauline's life experience—especially sex—has been defined in terms of color: the yellow of lemonade, the purple of berries. Now she is steeped in a profusion of "black-and-white images" which "[come] together, making a magnificent whole" (122). The "magnificent" synthesis of polar opposites apparently inherent in black-and-white film is a deception. As the tooth-loss failure of Pauline's Jean Harlow imitation demonstrates, conflation of black and white is impossible; the two must remain separate and opposite. Pauline decides that in the (white) "absolute scale of beauty" (122) her blackness is disgusting—and she "settles down to being ugly" (123). The disparity between black and white culminates in a linear hierarchy of power connecting pole to opposite pole: "White women said, 'Do this.' White children said, 'Give me that.' White men said, 'Come here.' Black men said, 'Lay down'" (138).

The distillation from diversity of color to black-and-white dichotomy effectively mirrors Pauline's tendency toward dry, rational simplification. Pauline claims that the advent of her children will bring peaceful coherence (126), but her eager internalization of dichotomy illustrates otherwise. Her process of "becoming" is one of simplification and deconstruction, not diversification; she "developed a hatred for things that mystified or obstructed her; acquired virtues that were easy to maintain; assigned herself a role in the scheme of things; and harked back to simpler times for gratification" (126). The narrator describes the lives of all black women as series of rich, wide-range paradoxes, careful tensions between homebound duties and social labor. They clear forests and deliver babies, butcher animals and nurture gardens, tend fields and sigh in their husbands' arms, "[pat] biscuits into flaky ovals of innocence—and [shroud] the dead" (138). Pauline rejects this spectrum of possibilities in favor of a simpler, Hollywood-defined set of binary opposites. She glories in her "flaky ovals of innocence" but repudiates household responsibilities; she internalizes a black-and-white polemical view of womanhood and places herself at one extreme of that polemic. Pauline's shift from diversity to dichotomy requires DuBoisian double consciousness, an awareness of both her actual and her perceived positions on any spectrum.

Pauline's double consciousness necessarily fashions a lifestyle as eminently asexual as "they" prescribe and deem worthy. She cannot attain whiteness, so she struggles against the boundaries of the controllable regions of her blackness. Pauline joins the "Geraldine movement" and seeks to blanch herself through quiet mental domination and sterile absolutism. Morrison chillingly describes the (a)sexuality of a Geraldinesque woman: "She will give him her body sparingly and partially. He must enter her surreptitiously, lifting the hem of her nightgown only to her navel. He must rest his weight on his elbows when they make love, ostensibly to avoid hurting her breasts but actually to keep her from having to touch or feel too much of him" (84). Pauline's asexuality, as apparent here, is characterized by a quasi-gnostic denial of—or at least disgust with—human physicality. Geraldine and Pauline, like Soaphead Church, reject contact with black humans as filthy and repulsive. They repudiate their own sexuality and practice a sort of mental self-castration, wishing that "the necessary but private parts of the body [were] in some more convenient place—like the armpit, for example, or the palm of the hand" (84). Pauline's "private world" at the Fishers' facilitates the fulfillment of lifelong dreams of bright order and cleanliness (128). The Fishers' color spectrum fits completely into whiteness; it is comprised of pink, white, and blue—and even engulfs the color composition of the "pink-and-yellow" Fishers themselves" (109). Because of a commitment to the white world's cleanliness, Pauline refuses to make contact with her own family's dirty environment. In self-defeating recognition of her blackness (i.e., ugliness), she rejects—gives up on—both her black body and her dirty home. Even the scant motherhood Pauline undertakes is a matter of "cleaning up;" she "[feels] she [is] fulfilling a mother's role conscientiously when she point[s] out their father's faults to keep them from having them, or punishe[s] them when they [show] any slovenliness, no matter how slight" (128-129). For Pauline, cleanliness is next to whiteness is next to godliness—and cleanliness entails separation from (black) physical reality.

The clean, funkless, sexless tradition of the girls from Mobile, Aiken, Marietta, and Meridian—a tradition of colorlessness and grim distinctions between black, white, ugly, and beautiful—is Pauline's inheritance, and she accepts it willingly. Her sex monologue ends with the only mildly nostalgic "Only thing I miss sometimes is that rainbow. But like I say, I don't recollect it much anymore" (131). Black/white dichotomy is a totalizing force, draining emotion, motivation, and color from her sexuality and rendering it an impotent element of her past. She has become a "mature woman for whom physical pleasure is only a memory" (Pettis 28)—and a distant memory, at that. Like Geraldine, she still participates in the sexual act, but as asexually as possible; according to Pecola, it is "as though she [is] not even there" (57). The personal presence previously associated with Pauline's sexuality gives way to absolute absence.

By distilling the spectra of her personhood and sexuality into a black-and-white binary, Morrison makes Pauline the picture of "womanhood in deterioration" (Pettis 28). The disintegration is comprehensive; once in place, the ideal of dichotomy runs rampant through Pauline's existence, confirming both her asexuality and her general fragmentation. She brittly distinguishes between beauty and ugliness; and her entrenchment in the white specular system of personhood determination renders her completely nonexistent (Walther 777). Pauline's separation of beauty from ugliness culminates in her treatment of her daughter, especially in the kitchen scene's physical polarization of Pauline's white charge and black Pecola. Indeed, "Pecola's ugliness is an affront to Pauline's surreptitious creation of beauty in the Fisher house" (Furman 17). Mother willingly rejects daughter in order to maintain the illusion of beauty.

Also particularly important to the erosion of Pauline's sexuality is her gnostic dichotomization of the earthly and spiritual. Pauline's sex monologue concludes with a resolute rejection of its legitimacy and beauty in favor of religious assurance: *"But I don't care 'bout it no more. My Maker will take care of me. I know He will. I know He will. Besides, it don't make no difference about this old earth. There is sure to be a glory"* (131). The rapturously-repeated "me" of the previous paragraph is displaced by the dryly spiritual "I know He will. I know He will;" Pauline's physical ecstasy gives way to desperate spirituality. In addition to black-vs.-white, beauty-vs.-ugliness, and earthly-vs.-spiritual, Pauline religiously distinguishes between cleanliness and filth, as in her attention to the two houses. She separates subject and object, objectifying Pecola in order to reduce the sting of her own hierarchical objectification. She dichotomizes hate and love, learning from the movies "all there [is] to love and...hate" (122). The character who previously reveled in the "rainbow" of her sexual and overall existence now hangs tenuously suspended above a series of black-and-white dichotomies. The reader hangs with her, surrounded by a shredded spectrum of questioned assumptions. Morrison, by masterfully bleeding color from Pauline's sexuality, harshly sketches the stark realities of a binary world.

## Works Cited

Furman, Jan. *Toni Morrison's Fiction.* Columbia: USC, 1996. Print.

Kuenz, Jane. "*The Bluest Eye*: Notes on History, Community, and Black Female Subjectivity." *African American Review 27* (1993): 421-431. Print.

Mack, Tracy. "Setting the Standards." *Chicago Tribune* 4 Apr. 2001, west final ed., sec. 8: 1+. Web.

Morrison, Toni. *The Bluest Eye.* New York: Vintage, 2000. Print.

Pettis, Joyce. "Difficult Survival: Mothers and Daughters in *The Bluest Eye*." *SAGE: A Scholarly Journal on Black Women* 4 (1987): 26-29. Print.

Walther, Malin LaVon. "Out of Sight: Toni Morrison's Revision of Beauty." *Black American Literature Forum* 24 (1990): 775-789. Print.

# What is Modernism?

**Literary modernism** is a term often used to describe the period between 1900 and 1940. "High modernism" is modernism at its peak, in the 1920s. It literature and art, it is usually characterized by experimental forms ("make it new"), aesthetic difficulty (especially due to allusiveness), interest in the individual's psychological experience, and a confidence that the masterpiece can help us to order the chaos that we have been left with after we lost confidence in the existence God.

## Different versions of modernism:

Modernism is far from monolithic. These two quotations show the specific concerns of these two writers, the first, a southerner, the second, a man from St. Louis, Missouri who eventually felt more at home in Europe.

### William Faulkner (Selected Letters of William Faulkner):

"I am telling the same story over and over, which is myself and the world. Tom Wolfe was trying to say everything, the world plus 'I' or filtered through 'I' to embrace the world in which he was born and walked a little while and then lay down again, into one volume. I am trying to go a step further. This I think accounts for what people call obscurity, the involved, formless 'style,' endless sentences. I am trying to say it all in one sentence, between one Cap and one period."

### T.S. Eliot, from "Tradition and the Individual Talent" (1920):

"The existing monuments form an ideal order among themselves, which is modified by the introduction of the new (the really new) work of art among them. The existing order is complete before the new work arrives; for order to persist after the supervention of novelty, the whole existing order must be, if ever so slightly, altered; and so the relations, proportions, values of each work of art toward the whole are readjusted; and this is conformity between the old and the new. Whoever has approved this idea of order, of the form of European, of English literature, will not find it preposterous that the past should be altered by the present as much as the present is directed by the past."

Here are some questions we will address in this class:

**\*How did World War II, the civil rights movement, the Vietnam war, Watergate, and other historical events affect American literature?**

**\*Which elements of modernism remain, and which get challenged? How?**

**\*What is postmodern literature? How and why did it develop?**

# Flannery O'Connor: Catholic Novelist

## 1. Early sources: Aquinas and neo-Thomists

St. Thomas Aquinas: "God cannot be seen in His essence by one who is merely man, except he be separated from this mortal life. The reason is, because, as was said above, the mode of knowledge follows the mode of the nature of the knower." (*Summa Theologica*, Q 12, Art 11).

## 2. Counterpoint: the Romantic theory of the imagination. (The "angelic imagination")

Ralph Waldo Emerson: "As fast as you conform your life to the pure idea in your mind, that will unfold its great proportions. A correspondent revolution in things will attend the influx of the spirit. So fast will disagreeable appearances, swine, spiders, snakes, pests, mad-houses, prisons, enemies, vanish; they shall be no more seen." (*Nature* 1836)

## 3. The Incarnational Logic of Fiction:

A. **It assumes the concrete world is good**:   St. Augustine wrote that the things of the world pour forth from God in a double way:  intellectually into the minds of the angels and physically into the world of things.  To the person who believes this---as the western world did up until a few centuries ago--this physical, sensible world is good because it proceeds from a divine source.  The artist usually knows this by instinct; his senses, which are used to penetrating the concrete, tell him so.  When Conrad said that his aim as an artist was to render the highest possible justice to the visible universe, he was speaking with the novelist's surest instinct. The artist penetrates the concrete world in order to find at its depths the image of its source, the image of ultimate reality. This in no way hinders his perception of evil but rather sharpens it, for only when the natural world is seen as good does evil become intelligible as a destructive force and a necessary result of our freedom (MM 157).

## B. It provides an encounter with--not an explanation of-- mystery:

Our sense of what is contained in our faith is deepened less by abstractions than by an encounter with mystery in what is human and often perverse. We Catholics are much given to the instant answer. Fiction doesn't have any. Saint Gregory wrote that every time the sacred text describes a fact, it reveals a mystery. And this is what the fiction writer, on his lower level, attempts to do also (*CW* 863).

## C. It can be a dirty job:

The fact is that the materials of the fiction writer are the humblest. Fiction is about everything human and we are made out of dust, and if you scorn getting yourself dusty, then you shouldn't try to write fiction. It's not a grand enough job for you (*MM* 68).

## D. It gives a different kind of knowledge:

To be great story-tellers, we need something to measure ourselves against, and this is what we conspicuously lack in this age. Men judge themselves now by what they find themselves doing. The Catholic has the teachings of the Church to serve him in this regard. But for the writing of fiction something more is necessary. For the purposes of fiction, these guides have to exist in the form of stories which affect our image and our judgment of ourselves. Abstractions, formulas, laws will not do here. We have to have stories. It takes a story to make a story. It takes a story of mythic dimensions; one which belongs to everybody; one in which everybody is able to recognize the hand of God and imagine its descent upon himself. In the Protestant South the Scriptures fill this role. The ancient Hebrew genius for making the absolute concrete has conditioned the Southerner's way of looking at things. That is one of the big reasons why the South is a story-telling section at all. Our response to life is different if we have been taught only a definition of faith than it is if we have trembled with Abraham as he held the knife over Isaac.  Both of these kinds of knowledge are necessary, but in the last four or five centuries we in the Church have over-emphasized the abstract and consequently impoverished our imagination and our capacity for prophetic insight.  The circumstance of being a Southerner, of living in a non-Catholic but religiously inclined society, furnishes the Catholic novelist with some very fine antidotes to his own worst tendencies (*CW* 858-9).

## 4. **The Power of the Grotesque.**

The novelist will have to do the best he can in travail with the world he has.  He may find that in the end that instead of reflecting the image at the heart of things, he has only reflected our broken condition and, through it, the face of the devil we are possessed by.  This is a modest achievement, but perhaps a necessary one  (*MM* 168).

Whenever I'm asked why Southern writers particularly have a penchant for writing about freaks, I say it is because we are still able to recognize one.  To be able to recognize a freak, you have to have some conception of the whole man, and in the South the general conception of man is still, in the main, theological  (*CW* 817).

When you can assume that your audience holds the same beliefs you do, you can relax a little and use more normal ways of talking to it; when you have to assume that it does not, then you have to make your vision apparent by shock--to the hard of hearing you shout, and for the almost blind you draw large and startling figures (*CW* 806).

## 5. **The Role of Violence**

I suppose the reasons for the use of so much violence in modern fiction will differ with each writer who uses it, but in my own stories I have found that violence is strangely capable of returning my characters to reality and preparing them to accept their moment of grace.  Their heads are so hard that almost nothing else will do the work.  This idea, that reality is something to which we must be returned at considerable cost, is one which is seldom understood by the casual reader, but it is one which is implicit in the Christian view of the world (*MM* 112).

*CW* = *The Collected Works of Flannery O'Connor*, Library of America edition

MM = *Mystery and Manners*, Sally and Robert Fitzgerald, ed. New York: Farrar, Straus, and Giroux, 1957.

Note: I have written a book on Flannery O'Connor: *The Incarnational Art of Flannery O'Connor*. Macon: Mercer UP, 2005.

# The Beat Generation

**Rough lecture outline:**

**1. Beat (the rhythm of the movement; its prose)**

**2. Beat ("up"...as in, on women...the feminist response)**

**3. Beat (beatific; spiritual aspects of the movement)**

## Defining "Beat"

"I meant beaten. The world against me."

-Herbert Huncke

"Call them hipsters, the 'beat generation,' 'postwar kids,' or our own displaced persons whatever you will."

- John Clellon Holmes

"Members of the generation that came of age after World War II, who, supposedly as a result of disillusionment stemming from the Cold War, espouse a mystical detachment and relaxation of social and sexual tensions."

-Jack Kerouac, his proposed definition of "Beat Generation" for the *Random House Dictionary*

"The point of Beat is that you get beat down to a certain nakedness where you actually are able to see the world in a visionary way, which is the old classical understanding of what happens in the dark night of the soul."

-Allen Ginsberg on the "beatific" quality of Beat

"By avoiding society you become separate from society and being separate from society is being Beat."

-Gregory Corso


Herb Caen coined the term "beatnik" after the October 1957 launching of the Russian "sputnik," asserting the satellite and the new bohemian type were equally "far-out."


"In the U.S. you have to be a deviant or die of boredom."

-William Burroughs

## 1950's:  the white suburban short story

As you would expect from a time of cultural homogenaeity, there will be a reflection of this in the literature.  And sure enough, the New critical movement does reflect this time well.

"New Criticism" refers to influential academics like Cleanth Brooks, a southerner, and others, many of them southern Christian gentlemen.  We talked about this movement briefly when I discussed O'Connor.  They represent both a way of reading fiction and a way of writing it.

They put a kind of faith in fiction, especially the short story and the poem, as a "well-wrought urn" a whole in of itself, complete, perfect structure, rising action, denoument, etc.  Poetry has ambiguity and mystery to be sure, but it all works together in the end masterfully, making the work beautiful.

The result:  if you are a college student in the 1950's, like Toni Morrison was, you are being taught the great masterworks of American Literature—like *Moby Dick*—as if they are the only important works in American literature, and almost as if you should worship them.

If you are writing in the 1950's and trying to get your stories published in the *New Yorker*, you are trying to write the GREAT AMERICAN NOVEL in the way that Hemingway was perceived to have done it; aggressively.  Kerouac had this in him, too, for all his bohemian ways.  If you can't write the great American novel, you are writing the "representative" story that speaks for all Americans, not realizing that "all" Americans means only white middle class educated readers of the *New Yorker*.  There was a lot of universalizing going on during this time, with little recognition of the margins.  That doesn't mean that the fiction was boring, or even racist-- only that it dealt somewhat exclusively with white, middle class suburban problems.

The writers: John Updike, John Cheever, Bernard Malamud

# The Black Arts Movement

The Black Arts movement is not identical to the Black Power movement, but they are related and do have similar goals. The Black Power movement was led largely by young black men in the late 1960s who were frustrated by the American government's empty promises of civil rights. Its fervor was fed by police brutality, racial profiling, the perception that blacks were sent in greater numbers to fight in Vietnam, and the conditions of inner city life (especially poverty). The Black Arts Movement was an aesthetic corollary to the Black Power Movement. It is believed to be started by the poet Amiri Baraka (LeRoi Jones), and its participants share the belief that art must be political and that it can change the world. It is centered around poetry and drama, whose public forms the artists felt could be used to incite energy for change.

It is a radical movement, in some ways insisting that African American literature of the past needs to be rethought. 1968, Maulana Karenga wrote that ". . .the blues are invalid; for they teach resignation, in a word acceptance of reality—and we have come to change reality. We will not submit to the resignation of our fathers who lost their money, their women, and their lives and sat around wondering 'what did they do to be so black and blue.' We will say again with brother LeRoi, 'We are lovers and the songs of lovers, and warriors and the sons of warriors.' Therefore we will love—and unwillingly though necessarily, make war, revolutionary war. We will not cry for those things that are gone, but find meaning in those things that remain with us."

It is a movement that wants nothing less than to revise the arts, which it considers to be ruined by white values. Also writing in 1968, Larry Neal explained that "it is the opinion of many Black writers, I among them, that the Western aesthetic has run its course: it is impossible to construct anything meaningful within its decaying structure. We advocate a cultural revolution in art and ideas. The cultural values inherent in western history must be either radicalized or destroyed."

# Post-structuralism

There is not enough time in this survey class to explain post-structuralism adequately, but the term "postmodern" cannot be understood without it. One quick thing to point out is that *post-structuralism* is a critique (of western philosophy as well as of structuralism); *deconstruction* is what someone with these convictions might do to a text; it is a type of reading. Deconstruction does not destroy the text; it simply illustrates how the text *undermines or subverts itself* because of the inherent slipperiness of language.

In the study of literature in America, three French figures have been the most influential. They are: **Roland Barthes** (especially his ideas about work vs. text and the death of the author); **Michel Foucault** (critiquing the way we have thought about knowledge); and **Jacques Derrida**. Derrida is perhaps the most well-known, and he is often vilified by people who have no idea what he is saying. He gave a famous lecture at Johns Hopkins University in 1966, called "Structure, Sign, and Play." In it he wrote that ". . .the entire history of the concept of structure, before the rupture of which we are speaking, must be thought of as a series of substitutions of centre for centre, as a linked chain of determinations of the centre. Successively, and in a regulated fashion, the centre receives different forms' or names. The history of metaphysics, like the history of the West, is the history of these metaphors and metonymies. Its matrix [. . .] is the determination of Being as *presence* in all senses of this word. It could be shown that all the names related to fundamentals, to principles, or to the centre have always designated an invariable presence – *eidos, archē, telos, energeia, ousia* (essence, existence, substance, subject) *alētheia*, transcendentality, consciousness, God, man, and so forth."

The center, that which we want so badly to be true, permanent, and transcendent, cannot hold and may be merely a linguistic construct.

# Metafiction

"Metafiction" is a term that was coined by the writer William Gass in the 1960s. The word plays upon the philosophical word "metaphysics." "Meta" means "after," so the term "metaphysics" means "after talking about physics." In this case, physics means Aristotle's works on physical matter. The word seems to suggest that after Aristotle worked out some ideas on what could be seen, he could then move to the deeper and more invisible questions, ultimate questions of reality, being, and the world. (Aristotle is considered the father of metaphysics). Topics include: the nature of the mind, philosophy of religion, the nature of time, and so on. The word "metaphysics" has also come to suggest "beyond" physical science, to the realm of the supernatural or transcendent.

So "metafiction" plays upon both senses of the word "meta." It is fiction that is *after* fiction, in the sense that it implies that conventional fiction is more or less dead, or at least, played out. More precisely, it designates that writing that is *beyond* or *above* fiction in that it is about writing itself, about *how* it generates meaning. It is fiction in which all the seams are showing, and all the "glory" is in the seams. Some of it is especially interested in showing the seams of the emperor's new clothes—in other words, showing that fiction is really only the seams after all. For some of these writers, there is no greater truth beyond the words and the tricks and the conventions of the writers themselves. In short, metafiction elevates the cleverness of the writer rather than the integrity of his work. Irony is its usual mode—and everything is subject to being ironized, or turned on its head in some way. Metafiction writers are especially adept at playing around with readers' expectations, expectations that have been generated by years of reading conventional fiction, years of being taught to read a certain way. Metafiction writers put this cultural training under pressure, and often push it until it shatters.

It thus loosely follows the critique that deconstruction offers of the whole idea of transcendence, especially in terms of how the New Critics saw the work of art as representing—indeed, reifying— "Truth" and "Beauty" in some nearly perfect way. Metafiction is interested in critiquing, exposing, or just making fun of how and why we read books the way we do. Mark Currie, in his book *Metafiction*, aptly called it "a kind of writing that takes place on the border between fiction and criticism, and which takes that border as its subject" (2).

Some keys to reading metafiction:

1.      Go with the flow. Let the writer play around a bit; that's what he or she is trying to do. (Think: *Shrek*).

2.      Ask yourself what sacred cows the writer seems to be milking and then harassing and/or killing.

3.      Note places in the text where the writer is especially self-conscious about the way that fiction works, especially the way that language works.

4.      I have found that I can tolerate self-conscious fiction best in extremely small doses. If you agree with me, you can thank me for not assigning Thomas Pynchon.

Writers in this vein especially include: William Gass, John Barth, Robert Coover. But lest you think that self-consciousness, seam-showing, and playing around with readers is new in fiction, you need to remember Chaucer's *Canterbury Tales* (1385); Cervantes' *Don Quixote* (1605); and especially Laurence Sterne's *Tristram Shandy* (1759).

# Toni Morrison

There is no doubt in my mind that Toni Morrison is the most important American writer of the second half of the 20th century. I could not imagine teaching this class without teaching her fiction.

The book *Conversations with Toni Morrison* is the source of the quotations that appear below.

1. When Morrison was **asked about her basic themes**, she replied that "...I think that I still write about the same thing, which is how people relate to one another and miss it or hang on to it...or are tenacious about love. About love and how to survive—not to make a living—but how to survive *whole* in a world where we are all of us, in some measure, *victims* of *something*. Each one of us is in some way at some moment a victim and in no position to do anything about it. Some child is always left unpicked up at some moment. In a world like that, how does one remain whole—is it just impossible to do that?" (40)

"Contemporary hostility to men is bothersome to me. Not that they are not deserving of criticism and contempt, but I don't want a freedom that depends largely on somebody else being on his knees. I also think that part of the women's complaint has to do with enormous expectations. The women like to say they are not dependent on love—as we said before—but there's so little left to love anyway—otherwise why make the man into opera, they make them into opera. What I'm trying to say is there was a time when you could love god, or your race, or your brother, or your sister, or your mother, but all those things have been taken from us in a way, because if you love god they think you are backward, if you love your mother they think you got some Freudian thing. . .And you could have a friend that you loved. Now if you have a friend that you love somebody will think that you are lesbian or homosexual. So what's left? There's nothing left to love, except the children and the member of the opposite sex. The person on the other end of that gets everything. It's too much; the lover expects so much from the beloved." (73)

2. Before she was a published novelist, Morrison was an editor for Random house in NYC, where she was responsible for bringing many talented black women writers into print. **When asked about what makes black literature "black",** Morrison replied that "I'm always a little disturbed by the sociological evaluations white people make of Black literature. Unless they are used as servants of aesthetics. I don't think it is possible to discuss a literature without taking into consideration what is sociologically or historically accurate, but most of the criticism in this country stops here. It's demoralizing for me to be required to explain Black life once again for the benefit of white people. Or to feel that I have to write about people who are 'typically Black.'" (67)

"Ralph Ellison and Richard Wright—all of whose books I admire enormously—I didn't feel were telling *me* something. I thought they were saying something about it or us that revealed something about us to you, to others, to white people, to men . . .there is a mask that sometimes exists when black people talk to white people. Somehow it seems to me that it spilled over into the fiction. I never thought that when I was reading black poetry, but when I began to write. When I wrote I wanted not to have to explain. Somehow, when black writers wrote for themselves I understood it better. What's the lovely line? When the locality is clear, fully realized, then it becomes universal." (96)

3. One of the things that makes Morrison such an incredible writer is her skill with language. She managed to capture what she thought was the difference in the way black people talk, but to do it in a way that is unmistakably Morrison. It was important to her to get it right, to let her prose sing. When asked about her **language**, Morrison said that "there is something different about that language [of Black people], as

there is about any cultural variation of English, but it's not saying 'dis' and 'dat.' It is the way words are put together, the metaphors, the rhythm, the music—that's the part of the language that is distinctly black to me when I hear it." (97).

When the interviewer asked, :"what makes it [your fiction] good?" Morrison replied, "The language, only the language. The language must be careful and must appear effortless. It must not sweat. It must suggest and be provocative at the same time. It is the thing that black people love so much— the saying of words, holding them on the tongue, experimenting with them, playing with them. It's a love, a passion. Its function is like a preacher's: to make you stand up out of your seat, make you lose yourself and hear yourself. The worst of all possible things that could happen would be to lose that language." (123)


"What you hear is what you remember. That oral quality is deliberate. It is not unique to my writing, but it is a deliberate sound that I try to catch. The way black people talk is not so much the use of a non-standard grammar as it is the manipulation of metaphor." (152)


"Oh yes, the image, the pictures, for me—it's what holds it. I can't move along in a chapter or part unless I can see the single thing that makes it clear—almost like a painting. As a matter of fact, in regard to your question about influences, I always think I am much more influenced by painters in my writing than by novelists. I can feel direct influences of painters. . .I think the language of Black people is just so full of metaphor and imagery—the way they talk is very concrete, is bright, and has a lot of color in it; has pictures. It's heavily loaded graphic-graphic. In addition to its sound, it has its sight—those two things." (179)


"I try to clean the language up and give words back their original meaning, not the one that's sabotaged by constant use, so that 'chaste' means what it meant originally. I try to do that by constructing sentences that throw such words into relief, but not strange words, not 'large' words. Most large words are imprecise. They are useful because of their imprecision. If you work very carefully, you can clean up ordinary words and repolish them, make parabolic language seem alive again." (165)

# Richard Wilbur

**Richard Wilbur** is considered one of the greatest American masters of poetic form, following in the footsteps of such great writers as Robert Frost, who famously said that writing free verse was like trying to "play tennis without a net." Wilbur himself is probably not that dogmatic about free verse, but he does see it as more limited in what it is able to accomplish. Because the poet **William Carlos Williams** is the most influential poet to champion the so-called "open forms," Wilbur is asked about him a lot. Wilbur has always had respect for Williams, though he often disagrees with him. Wilbur said of Williams that "he was always warm when we met, and told me to call him Bill, and was generous about my poems despite his theoretical disapproval. My feeling about meters and forms generally is that for a good poet—a poet who has the strength to take them over—they are undated and indeed timeless. For such a poet, they are simply instruments or contraption which heighten and empower his words—underlining the shape and steps of the argument, giving it an appropriate music, honing the colloquial movement, hitting the important words hard, changing the utterance in every way."

In 1999, *The Atlantic Monthly* interviewed the poet Richard Wilbur. In 1995, the journal *Image* had interviewed him. Some of his thoughts are below.


1. When asked about how **he feels about "perfection in form,"** Wilbur remarked that, "as a fancier of motion, physical motion in poetry, I am always a little put off by the word "perfection," which suggests immobility to me. I have never aimed at a monumental quality in my poems, and I don't much like it in the poems of others. It pleases me always to endanger whatever form I'm working in. I've written very few sonnets, but when I work in the sonnet, I try to threaten the form, expressively, in the way that my hero John Milton always did. Milton's sonnets freely overrun the tidy divisions

of the sonnet form for expressive purposes, and therefore if his poems are "perfect," they're not perfect in the sense of being neat. They're perfect in the sense of treating the form in such a way as at all times to put it at the service of the meaning."

2. When asked **how the form directs the energy of the poem**, Wilbur sad that "I must say that I never think of form as *directing*. I don't think of the form itself as making any demands. In this I suppose I'm very close to being a free-verse poet. I think of the form as something that you choose because what you want to say is going to be able to take advantage of it. One example that I have always given my students is the Petrarchan sonnet. Robert Frost used to say if you have something you'd like to say for about eight lines and then want to take it back for six lines, you're on the verge of writing a sonnet. And he meant the Petrarchan, I guess, in that case. Every form I think has a certain logic, has certain expressive capabilities. Most of the time the ideas that come to us have no business at all being thrust into the sonnet form. If we did start behaving that way, it would be true that the form would be directing us, would be making certain demands. But if one chooses form rightly, one is not submitting to the demands of the form but making use of it at every moment."

3. When asked whether or not **versification provides a "constant reengagement with the artistry of the past,"** Wilbur said that the person who said that, Douglas Dunn, "may be close to saying something I always object to that William Carlos Williams said. I love Bill Williams's poems, but his critical opinions seem to me to be nonsense. He was forever saying that if you write a sonnet you are making a curtsey to the court of Queen Elizabeth I -- that if you wrote a sonnet nowadays your language would inevitably be invaded by Elizabethan language and you would find yourself employing Elizabethan themes. I think that was probably so for him. I think that is one reason why he had to write as he did and stay away from the sonnet."

4. When asked what he thinks about the whole **free-verse movement**, and **whether or not something is lost in it,** Wilbur said that "I suppose that I'm capable of responding to the minimal excitements of free verse because I've read so much of it. When I say the minimal excitement, I meant that there isn't much formal force in most free verse except for the supposed tension that occurs by the breaking of the line. . .I think that in free verse one loses all sorts of opportunities for power, emphasis and precision, especially in rhythmic precision. If you read the poems of Robert Frost, above all the *North of Boston* poems, you hear the New England voice speaking in its native rhythm. Because there's a loose iambic pentameter going on, you can't misread those poems. You can't fail to read them as if you were a New Englander. Now if someone attempts a poetry of distinctive speech rhythms without a metrical base, I think a good part of the intended emphasis is going to get away."

5. When asked about **his thoughts regarding the confessional or autobiographical mode of poetry**, Wilbur said that "I am of two minds about the confessional mode. A poem as classy as Lowell's 'Skunk Hour' goes far toward justifying it, and I could make a list of admirable unburdenings by W.D. Snodgrass, John Berryman, and other able poets who, in whatever mode they chose to write, would write well. It must be said, however, that confessional writing can conduce, even in the best, to self-dramatization and celebrity posturing, neither of which make for good poems. Confessional poets of real talent should not perhaps be blamed for inspiring the sort of dismal creative-writing poem we have been seeing for three decades: slack, prosaic, self-absorbed, merely personal. Poems *have* to be based in autobiography; how else should they come about? But if they are to be of any use, they must end by being about everybody. I think of Edwin Muir's poems, which arise from intense personal memories and yet modulate into universal myth."

6.  When asked about his **belief in God, how Christianity informs his poetry,** and where he would fit on an arc between Gerard Manley Hopkins and T. S. Eliot, Wilbur said that "I think I belong at the Hopkins end of that arc because I'm the sort of Christian animal for whom celebration is the most important thing of all. I know that, as you say, there is terror in my poems, not so much presented as a tangible scariness but as a felling that the order of things is in peril or in doubt, that there are holes in things through which one might drop for a long distance. The terror is there and it's countered continually by trust and by hope, but an impulse to praise. When I go to church, what doesn't particularly interest me is the Creed, although I find I can say it. The Creed strikes me as very much like a political platform of some sort, and I believe that's what it was. What I respond to is, 'Lift up your hearts!' It's lines like that in the Mass that belong to me, belong to my kind of religious experience."

7.  When asked if he has a **sacramental vision of the world,** Wilbur replied: "Yes. As Fr. Hopkins says, 'The world is charged with the grandeur of God.' I don't often preach, and I don't often quote myself either, but I think that what Hopkins says is implied in certain of my more declarative lines: 'We invent nothing....' And: 'The world's fullness is not made but found.'"

# Don DeLillo: context for discussion

1. Jacques Ellul, *The Humiliation of the Word* (1981)

Ellul is a Christian writer whose primary concern is the ascendancy of technique in the modern world. "Technique," according to him, is any tool employed by society, in every realm, to achieve greater efficiency. In *The Humiliation of the Word*, he explains that technique rules by way of the image, and that the image has humiliated the word in modern life.

He makes the following associations:

**Image – Reality – Seeing**

**Word – Truth – Hearing**

Ellul argues that word and image belong to two different *modes* of thought. One is not superior to the other, but society has allowed image to trump the word to incredible deleterious effects, including the devaluation and degradation of the word and word-oriented thinking in general. Television is one of the places where this is most clearly seen. Television images, he argues, monopolize us, and give us a false reality that we nonetheless live inside of. "Thus the reality I see, and to which I am urged to dedicate myself, is a false reality. . . since I know that images no longer refer to anything, I am led to choose from among the floods of images those that are easiest to understand, instead of those which could have rich meaning. The result is that we are faced not only with a false reconstructed reality and a false relationship with reality because of mediation by images, but also with a false language" (146).

2. Walter Benjamin, "The Work of Art in the Age of Mechanical Reproduction" (1935)

"One might subsume the eliminated element in the term 'aura' and go on to say: that which withers in the age of mechanical reproduction is the aura of the work of art. This is a symptomatic process whose significance points beyond the realm of art. One might generalize by saying: the technique of reproduction detaches the reproduced object from the domain of tradition. By making many reproductions it substitutes a plurality of copies for a unique existence. And in permitting the reproduction to meet the beholder or listener in his own particular situation, it reactivates the object reproduced. These two processes lead to a tremendous shattering of tradition which is the obverse of the contemporary crisis and renewal of mankind. Both processes are intimately connected with the contemporary mass movements. Their most powerful agent is the film. Its social significance, particularly in its most positive form, is inconceivable without its destructive, cathartic aspect, that is, the liquidation of the traditional value of the cultural heritage .
. ."

3. David Harvey "The Condition of Postmodernity" (1989)

"The whole world's cuisine is now assembled in one place in almost exactly the same way that the world's geographical complexity is nightly reduced to a series of images on a static television screen. This same phenomenon is exploited in entertainment places like Epcott and Disneyworld; it becomes possible, as the US commercials put it, 'to experience the Old World for a day without actually having to go there.' The general implication is that through the experience of everything from food, to culinary habits, music, television, entertainment, and cinema, it is now possible to experience the world's geography vicariously, as a simulacrum. The interweaving of simulacra in daily life brings together different worlds (of commodities) in the same space and time. But it does so in such a way as to conceal almost perfectly any trace of origin, of the labour processes that produced them, or of the social relations implicated in their production.

The simulacra can in turn become the reality. Baudrillard (1986) in *L'Amerique* even goes so far, somewhat exaggeratedly in my view, to suggest that US reality is now constructed as a giant screen: 'the cinema is everywhere, most of all in the city, incessant and marvelous film and scenario.' Places portrayed in a certain way, particularly if they have the capacity to attract tourists, may begin to 'dress themselves up' as the fantasy images prescribe."

4. Soren Kierkegaard *The Sickness Unto Death* (1849)

"What is really missing is the strength to obey, to yield to the necessary in one's self, what might be called one's limits. Nor therefore is it the misfortune of such a self not to have become anything in the world; no, the misfortune is that he did not become aware of himself, that the self he is is a quite definite something, and thus the necessary. Instead, through this self's fantastically reflecting itself in possibility, he lost himself. Even to see one*self* in a mirror one must recognize oneself, for unless one does that, one does not see one*self*, only a human being. But the mirror of possibility is no ordinary mirror; it must be used with the utmost caution. For in this case the mirror is, in the highest sense, a false one. The fact that in the possibility of itself a self appears in such and such a guise is only half-truth; for in the possibility of itself the self is still far from, or only half of, itself."

# Sandra Cisneros

Sandra Cisneros is perhaps the most well-known and well-respected of Chicana writers alive today. Cisneros was born in Chicago in 1954, and was raised on the south side. Cisneros was one of the writers who—arguably even more than Toni Morrison—had to make her own way in the absence of any models for her writing. She is dedicated to telling the story from her perspective, and working to speak for Mexican Americans like herself who would be otherwise voiceless. She is especially interested in letting Latina women speak, because in the culture generally, women are expected only to get married and to raise a family, not to become professional writers.

1. When asked about **why she writes**, Cisneros reflected that "I'm trying to write the stories that haven't been written. I felt like a cartographer; I'm determined to fill a literary void. [. . .] One of the most frightening pressures I faced as I wrote this book [Mango Street]. . .was the fear that I would blow it....I kept asking myself, What have I taken on here? That's why I was so obsessed with getting everybody's stories out."

2. When asked about how she **felt about her upbringing** and how it **contributes to her literary voice**, Cisneros said that "As a poor person growing up in a society where the class norm was superimposed on a tv screen, I couldn't understand why our home wasn't all green lawn and white wood. . . I rejected what was at hand and emulated the voices of the poets. . . big, male voices. . .all wrong for me. . .it seems crazy but. . .I had never felt my home, family, and neighborhood unique or worthy of writing about."

3. When **asked about marriage**, Cisneros said that "I have some friends who are married and they seem to be happy, but I can't imagine myself in that kind of relationship. I really like my solitude. I don't like being lonely, but I'm not lonely. I

need to be alone to work. I have very close friends and very close men in my life, but I don't want them in my house. That's the difference. . .My writing is my child and I don't want anything to come between us. I like to know that if I come home very late from teaching—and teaching is exhausting, as exhausting as factory work, except I work more hours and get paid more—I don't want to come home to a husband. I want to come home to my books, and if I want to, I want to be alone to think. As a writer you need time to think, even if you're not writing. . .I wish we had little lights on our forehead like confessionals had. When someone was inside, the little light used to go red: "Ocupado." I want one like that: "Don't bother me, I'm thinking." Some men do respect that. But people cannot read your mind and know that you are thinking even though you're not writing....When I'm living with a man, he becomes my project. Like it or not, you find yourself doing it, then you get angry at yourself. I know that I'm difficult to live with. I like my loneness, and I think that's the way I work best."

## Poetry: Open forms (Black Mountain, Objectivists, Deep Image, New York school, Beats, etc.)

Literary ancestor: William Carlos Williams

Besides the literary innovations of William Carlos Williams, the most important piece of writing was **Charles Olsen's "Projected Verse" of 1950**, which was said to be the inspiration and the manifesto for the Black Mountain school of poetry.

According to Olsen, the new open forms must displace the old, closed forms, which are tired. A poet learns that a poem is "high energy-construct" that discharges that energy to the reader. The principle is that "FORM IS NEVER MORE THAN AN EXTENSION OF CONTENT. (Or so it got phrased by one, R. Creely, and it makes absolute sense to me. . .)." One perception should lead to another, says Olsen, and that means "get on with it, keep moving, keep in, speed, the nerves, their speed, the perceptions, theirs, the acts, the split second acts, the whole business, keep it moving as fast as you can, citizen."

"I take it that PROJECTIVE VERSE teaches, is, this lesson, that that verse will only do in which a poet manages to register both the acquisitions of his ear *and* the pressures of his breath." Breath is so important to Olsen that he says that the *syllable is king*.

**Robert Duncan (Black Mountain):** "A longing grows to return to the open composition in which the accidents and imperfections of speech might awake intimations of human being."

**Louis Zukofsky (Objectivists):** "An objective: (optics)-The lens bringing the rays from an object into focus. That which is aimed at. (Use extended to poetry) – Desire for what is objectively perfect, inextricably the direction of historic and contemporary particulars."

**Charles Wright (speaking as reader of Deep Image):** "Poetry is important for what is not said as for what is. The secret of poetry is silence, the unheard echoes of utterances that wash through us with their solitary innuendos."

# Andre Dubus

Andre Dubus is not the most well-known of writers, and perhaps the biggest reason for that is that he is a master of the short story, which is a tough literary nut to crack when it comes to getting recognized. But for Christians, he is one of the most important literary models we have. He was born and raised Louisiana, and spent most of his life in Massachusetts. A cradle Catholic, Dubus's faith has informed his entire life's work, especially in terms of his moral vision. He was hit by a car in 1986 while helping a motorist. He lost one leg and the use of the other, and gained a sharpened focus for his writing. Most of the following quotations come from a 1987 interview.

(For an article I wrote on Dubus called "Living Like a Man: Andre Dubus and the Lessons of Brokenness" see *Books and Culture*, May 2003. http://www.ctlibrary.com/bc/2003/mayjun/6.8.html.)

1. When asked whether he sees "**any resemblance between [your work] and James Joyce's** *A Portrait of the Artist as a Young Man*," Dubus said: "God, I hope there's none. . .There is no love, no heart [in Joyce]. As I recall, he wrote to his brother from Trieste, "I'm getting back at them for what they did to me." So he writes about Irish clerks made spiritually impotent by poverty, Catholicism, overbearing clergy, and dominating women. I said to Richard Yates once, "You know, you once said in an interview that the two problems of fictional autobiography were self-pity and self-aggrandizement. What do you think about a book that starts with a boy in bed and ends with him becoming the conscience of the cosmos?" He said, "I think Joyce violated both those rules." As you see, I can't stand Joyce. I have not read anything of his for a long time. I think he was a self-absorbed son of a bitch. . .so I hope there are no parallels between our approaches to writing and the sacred."

2. When asked where he **places himself in the literary tradition**, and **what were his influences**, Dubus said "I guess I am a realist. It is nothing I ever think about except

when I'm reading a book that is not real [laughs]. I do not like to read books that do not have characters in them. If I cannot become the character in the book I am reading, I quickly lose interest, and I've stopped reading novels because the day after the night I was reading, I find I'm not worried about the people, so I just do not go back to the book. I do not see myself descending from any line of writers because I do not clearly see a line. I am certainly vastly influenced by Chekhov and, of course, Hemingway, who is not a realist—anybody who says he is a realist does not know how to read Hemingway. But Chekhov is the one I look up to the most. I majored in literature, but I do not remember if there is a *line,* and I sort of doubt that there is one. I think it is a game teachers play so they can have a package. 'In this six weeks we'll cover this line of writers,' and that takes care of that, as though they are studying evolution. I don't think it's that simple."

"I learned the most when I was young from Hemingway and a lot of that was physical stuff. Stopping a sentence in midline. Stopping your work for the day when you're still going well. Exercising afterwards and trying never to think about your work when you are still going well. Exercising afterwards and trying never to think about your work when you are not actually at the desk. Hemingway inspired my romantic side when I was eighteen or nineteen. I thought it would be great to walk around with a beret and go to bullfights and shit like that. But my major influence is Anton Chekhov. I think a trace of Faulkner comes into my prose sometimes, but Chekhov is the one who really grabbed my heart and kept it. Because of how much he could get done in so little. Nobody can touch him when he goes over twenty-five pages."

3. When asked "What is **your opinion of the so-called new fiction, metafiction, superfiction, surfiction, bossa nova,** etc.,.?" Dubus replied: "Well, these are writers I can't read. I have tried them all. I did like Coover's baseball book. It did not make me want to read any more Coover. I read two or three of Barthelme's books, and I gave up. Read some of Gass, gave up. I read *The End of the Road* by Barth, loved it, and then taught it and got angry. Seemed to me that in the

abortion scene when she drowns in her own vomit, that we should have been weeping, and I don't like the comic distance, so I've never read a word of his since. But I can't call these people assholes because they write something that they feel, but I don't feel, something they like, but I don't like. I don't like their work, but I certainly respect their *doing* it. There is no way to criticize these people. I can't think they're phonies. I don't think they're dishonest. I think they are real artists. They work hard, and they are just doing something that doesn't interest me."

 Raymond Carver 1938-1988

*Practitioner of what is sometimes called "minimalism" or "designer fiction" or "dirty fiction"

*John Barth called anything that was written in Carver's wake "Post-Alcoholic Blue-Collar Minimalist Hyperrealism"

*Inheritor of Ernest Hemingway's so-called "iceberg theory" of writing:

"If a writer of prose knows enough about what he is writing about he may omit things that he knows and the reader, if the writer is writing truly enough, will have a feeling of those things as strongly as though the writer had stated them. The dignity of movement of the iceberg is due to only one-eighth of it being above water. The writer who omits things because he does not know them only makes hollow places in his writing." [from *Death in the Afternoon*]

## Blogger rolls dice to create really, really short stories

By April Dembosky • SACRAMENTO BEE

December 29, 2009

For a writer, Jason Sinclair Long is obsessed with numbers. Before he types a word, he rolls a pair of dice, one green, one gray, both eight-sided relics from pre-teen Dungeons and Dragons bouts.

Shake. Toss. Sigh. Write.

He tells the story of a murder in 31 words. A marriage in 87. A sci-fi ditty in 12. Or a travel adventure in 63. The lower the number, usually, the longer he spends in front of his laptop. "I fear the elevens," said Long, 37, of Auburn, Calif. "Sometimes a very, very short story takes an hour or two, in some cases more, because I labor over word choice and sentence structure."

Long started his project, Flash Fiction 365, on Jan. 1 this year. He was inspired by the six-word story, attributed to Ernest Hemingway, *For sale: baby shoes, never worn,* and a schedule increasingly packed with teaching and raising his toddler son. Long set out to write and post one very short story on his blog every day until Dec. 31. It could be any genre, between 11 and 88 words long. Titles don't count toward the word total. The results sometimes read like experimental poetry. Underneath each tale, Long has held himself to the rules of short-story composition: Each must contain an exposition, characters, plot and setting. There must be some kind of conflict that arcs into a climax, then resolves in denouement. "I'm not always able to do it," Long said. "That's the thing about doing it every day. You miss, miss, miss, miss, and then you hit. Then you miss again."

On Feb. 23, Long rolled an 88 and wrote a hit, called "Balancing Racks":

Victor couldn't remember the last time Stella wanted to play Scrabble period, let alone all night.

Next morning, dead even, they ignored their glassy-eyed stares and went one more.

Stella triple-worded her way to victory.

"Feeling superior?" V asked.

She hummed lightly, smiling in reply.

He boxed the game, shelved it, brewed Darjeeling.

She opened a window, let in the air.

"I cheated," Stella said, at last.

"I know."

"Not at Scrabble."

"I know."

They held their tea close, warming their hands against the worst of it.


\*\*\*\*\*\*\*\*\*

# Guidelines: graded class discussion

The graded class discussion takes the place (along with the BIR) of a longer paper that would have been due at the end of the semester). It is a skills test that will discern how well you can:

1. converse about literature (use terms, etc.)
2. work in a group setting to advance the group
3. situate the work within the themes of the class
4. bring in helpful outside research

I will remain completely silent (believe it or not I can do this!) through the entire period. You and your group will be responsible for planning and organizing how the discussion will go: who will ask questions and/or otherwise direct? (this can be shared) Who will bring in some outside research to illuminate the group with relevant materials? How can you make sure that the silent members of the group have a chance to participate? How can you make sure you hit the salient parts of the text?

You will be graded according to the following criteria:

1. The quality of your individual contributions to the class discussion. Did your comments help or hinder the overall discussion? Part of what I am testing you on is your judgment of what kinds of comments are relevant and interesting in a good literary discussion.

2. Whether or not you spoke too much or too little. Are you dominating the discussion, or are you barely involved? Strive for something between those two poles.

3. How well the group does as a whole. Did everyone feel able to participate? Was the discussion enlightening for everyone, or did it feel like a rehash of the obvious?

# How to study for and take a Bieber Lake final

To study:

1.     Proceed chronologically.  Re-read useful introductory material for what you review; make notes of helpful themes, dates, ideas.

2.     Make sure you memorize names of writers and their corresponding works that we read.  Observe things about those works that will help you identify them:  diction, style, structure, point of view, tone, punctuation/capitalization, etc.

3.     With your lecture/discussion notes (and this book) in hand, review the selections we read, slowing down over passages you marked or that we discussed in class.  Any time you hit upon what you think is a major theme of the course, write it down.  Consider the writer's ideas as well as his or her aesthetic choices—you will need to address both.

4.     Make sure you re-familiarize yourself with the main characteristics of the overall piece you are studying:  what were its main arguments? What were some telling scenes? What kinds of metaphors did the poet often use? And so on. The more of these you memorize and can pull into your essays (even if they are not in the quotation itself), the better.

On the test day:

1.     Bring loose leaf paper and a smooth pen.  Write on one side of the paper only. *Write legibly or I will give you no credit for your answers.*

2.     *Do not spend more than about 15 minutes* on the identification section. Return at the end of the exam to some quotations that you were not sure of.  The more quickly you can move through this section, the more time you have to think about and develop your essays.

---

3.      Spend *at least 15 minutes* selecting the column and quotations you will address. Be careful: choose a quotation you feel you can say something interesting about over a quotation that is very familiar to you but leads to dead-end thought. Advanced students: think about writing about quotations that others are not as likely to choose.

4.      Be careful to write a brief outline before you begin. Do not forget to *think*. Sounds obvious, but given the time constraints, it is often better to make a few notes to yourself and then write out the *best* of them than it is to think on paper when you do not have time to revise.

5.      Make sure your essay contains each of the following (integrated in your answer): 1. Briefly quoted (or referred to) words/images from the quotation that illustrate that you understand what is written there and can use it to support your answer. 2. A contextualization of that passage in the larger work. An excellent answer will also draw in other relevant scenes, images, or ideas from the work. 3. Some discussion of the work as an *aesthetic* work—its structure, word choice, rhyme scheme, intended audience, tone, etc—and how those things contribute to the argument/theme you address. 4. A relation (usually comparison/contrast) of the two or three quotations to each other and to larger issues of the course.

6.      Relax! You've worked hard: enjoy the act of expressing what you have learned!

Made in the USA
San Bernardino, CA
22 December 2017